MW01484074

THE STOCK PHOTOGRAPHY HANDBOOK

How to create passive income through stock photography

JETT PARKER-HOLLAND

ABSTRACT PRESS

Contents

Stock photography as passive income   3

    The passive income model   3

    What is stock photography?   4

    An Experiment: 10 years as a stock photographer   10

How to get started in stock photography   17

    Equipment   18

    Software   35

    Photography training   39

How to create stock photography that sells   43

    General Rules   45

    Popular categories   48

    Postprocessing   73

How to optimise your stock photography process   77

    Stock Photography Agencies   78

    Metadata   83

    Rejections   86

THE STOCK PHOTOGRAPHY HANDBOOK

How to create passive income through stock photography

Stock photography as passive income

The passive income model

Passive income is the focus of many entrepreneurs, and while the concept has been around for centuries it is now far more accessible to the ordinary person. Passive income is just that, passive, it means that whether you're at work, asleep or watching tv you are still generating an income without having to lift a finger. With passive income, you create your investment, and then leave it to generate money, this can help remove your dependency on a regular 9-5 job and enjoy a greater sense of financial security. Passive income requires an initial investment that will provide multiple earnings over time; these investments can be either monetary (by investing in bonds or income generating stocks), or an investment in time (such as stock photography).

The passive income model focuses on having multiple streams of income, many experts recommend at least 5 distinct streams of income, but everyone has to start with one. If you are still new to passive income, stock photography is a very beginner friendly way to begin your passive income portfolio. It's important to remember that you should ultimately seek to have multiple sources of passive income to reduce your risk of being exposed to any one income stream[1]. This shouldn't scare you, only keep in mind that the model of passive income works best when you have several effective sources of income.

In this book we will be showing you how to maximise your income from stock photography and how to maximise your return on your time investment.

What is stock photography?

At its essence, stock photography is where a photographer creates an image and then sell it later. This is different to the traditional income model for photographers, where images would be commissioned or requested in advance. When we talk about stock photography[2] we tend to think of 'microstock'. Microstock is where a photographer makes their images available as a royalty-free license, this means that the customer buys a license to use the image however they

---

[1] For example, a financial crisis could reduce the profitability of all income stocks, or a large source of royalty free images could reduce the value of all stock photographs.

[2] Specifically, when we refer to stock photography in this book.

like. This type of stock photography will be the focus of this book.

Traditionally, stock photography involved the selling of the full rights of ownership of an image to the buyer[3]. Stock photography was also available as "rights managed" images which allowed the purchaser to use the image under specific conditions. This is the traditional market for stock photography and is often referred to as 'macrostock'. Macrostock has become a much smaller market since the introduction of microstock and is only accessible to photographers that use high-end equipment and have a strong personal brand. This area of stock photography is not the focus of this book but is another form of stock photography that you may encounter.

Other types of stock

Editorial

Editorial stock photography[4] is an area of microstock which caters to the needs of media outlets. These images differ from normal stock photography as the images may contain identifiable logos or people. On the whole these images sell for a much higher price than normal

---

[3] This was often in the range of hundreds or thousands of dollars.
[4] Usually just called 'editorial'.

stock photography, but because these images are intended for websites and newspapers, there are far fewer images that are appropriate for editorial. Editorial photos also tend to sell in much lower quantities as they are usually only relevant for a particular piece of news. Editorial photos do sell, but never in high quantities, they also don't generate repeat sales which makes them only profitable in the short time they are relevant. While this can generate earnings for the photographer it does not fit in with the passive income model.

Editorial may be an area that you wish to explore and may be appropriate if you are able to shoot at a place where there is an interesting event or location[5] but this often requires being in specific and competitive locations. Because of this editorial requires a lot of time and effort to produce photos that will only sell for a short amount of time; this has the effect of essentially translating time into money. For this reason, there are many professional photographers that specialise in editorial as a profession, but this association with converting time to money and the lack of ongoing sales means that this is not appropriate for the passive income model.

---

[5] E.g. in Munich for Oktoberfest, or in Rio de Janeiro for Carnival.

6

Stock footage

Stock footage is very similar to stock photography except that is focuses on video content rather than image content. Once you are familiar with the process of creating stock photography that sells well you may consider moving into stock footage as this is an area that still enjoys higher earnings per download and less competition than traditional stock photography. You may wish to wait until you are confident in stock photography before moving on to stock footage as there are different skills and equipment that you will need to be successful: Firstly, you will need photography equipment that is capable of producing high quality video as the video setting on many entry-level DSLRs will not be good enough for stock footage. You will also need purchase, and be comfortable in using, video editing software as stock footage requires a significantly greater amount of editing. Stock footage does not fall within the scope of this book but is an excellent addition to the passive income model and is recommended as an effective way to expand your portfolio.

Stock illustration

Stock illustration sells very well. This area focuses on artwork that is created to be used in different commercial applications. Because these designs require an artist to create them, there is less competition in this market and allows for a greater amount of differentiation. Stock illustration also requires a certain amount of creativity and artistry that many people do not have. If you have skills in drawing or graphic design, then this is an area that may suit you. To create stock illustration, you will need to have different software to stock photography, but with a little extra investment this can create a strong addition to your passive income portfolio.

What to expect from stock photography

Stock photography is a very competitive market. Originally only professional photographers were involved in the creation of stock photography and it was definitely a seller's market. Since then many people have entered the stock photography market and competition is fierce, anyone with a smartphone can essentially become a stock photographer (but many will not become successful). The good news is that as the technology has advanced more and more people need stock photography for their projects, and the majority of stock images on the market are of a very poor quality. If you can produce good quality images you will have eliminated the majority of your competition.

At the time of writing, the biggest and most popular stock photography agency is Shutterstock. Shutterstock has over 250 million images available for sale, with about 1.3 million images added weekly. Most of the images added are of poor quality and there is still a strong market for well-produced photographs. The good and bad news is that in the 10 years that stock photography has been popular, many of the photos uploaded are still relevant. This means that images that are over a decade old are still competing for new sales, however, this also means that any well produced images that you contribute still have the potential to sell and generate earnings indefinitely; this is what makes stock photography so useful for the passive income model.

While earnings differ from agency to agency, contributors receive approximately $0.50 per download on Shutterstock, and many contributors will quote an average income of $1 per image per year. Therefore, a well-diversified stock portfolio of 1,200 images should produce an average income of $100 per month. You can also expect to have good and bad months as a stock contributor, in some cases this will be because some images are seasonal (such as Christmas photos), and other times this can occur just through chance. Similarly, some areas of photography have a shorter shelf life than others[6].

An Experiment: 10 years as a stock photographer

This book aims to show how stock photography can be a viable passive income stream. As mentioned before, many contributors will agree that average earnings of $1 per image per year is an achievable target for a stock photographer.

It isn't expected that you will quit your current income to become a dedicated stock photographer, but a contribution of 100 images per month to your stock portfolio is achievable with anyone's schedule.

The first 2 years

Following this model, if we assume that your stock portfolio will produce $1 per image per year and you contribute 100 images per month to your stock portfolio, you can expect to create a portfolio that grows with each passing month. At the end of the second year you will have a portfolio of 2,400 images, generating $200 per month, on average. Following this model, you can

---

[6] Images of objects stay relevant a lot longer than images of people or technology that can become outdated as trends come and go.

expect your cumulative income for the first 2 years to look like this:

2-Year Cumulative income

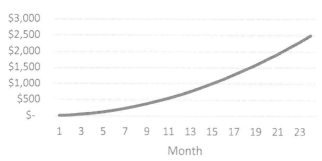

Your first 24 months of income would look
similar to this:

Month	Portfolio size	Revenue	Cumulative income
1	100	$ 8.33	$ 8
2	200	$ 16.67	$ 25
3	300	$ 25.00	$ 50
4	400	$ 33.33	$ 83
5	500	$ 41.67	$ 125
6	600	$ 50.00	$ 175
7	700	$ 58.33	$ 233
8	800	$ 66.67	$ 300
9	900	$ 75.00	$ 375
10	1000	$ 83.33	$ 458
11	1100	$ 91.67	$ 550
12	1200	$ 100.00	$ 650
13	1300	$ 108.33	$ 758
14	1400	$ 116.67	$ 875
15	1500	$ 125.00	$ 1,000
16	1600	$ 133.33	$ 1,133
17	1700	$ 141.67	$ 1,275
18	1800	$ 150.00	$ 1,425
19	1900	$ 158.33	$ 1,583
20	2000	$ 166.67	$ 1,750
21	2100	$ 175.00	$ 1,925
22	2200	$ 183.33	$ 2,108
23	2300	$ 191.67	$ 2,300
24	2400	$ 200.00	$ 2,500

If after 2 years you no longer wanted to produce
any more photographs for stock photography,
you would have created already created $2,500
in additional income over those first 2 years. But
the great thing about passive income is that your
portfolio continues to generate income even if you
no longer contribute to it. Even if you no longer
produced any more stock photography after the
first 2 years, by the end of the 5th year you would
have generated $9,700.

The first 10 years

Let's continue with this example and say that you didn't want to contribute to your stock portfolio after the first 2 years. Your portfolio would continue to generate income, and after 10 years you would have created a total of $21,700. All for the work of producing 100 images per month for 2 years.

If you had continued producing 100 images a month for the full 10 years[7], you would have a portfolio of 12,000 images producing $1,000 per month, having earned a total of $60,500 over that period. That's an average of $504 per month over the 10 years[8].

---

[7] It's difficult to make predictions about stock photography more than 10 years in the future, as this is roughly as long as the stock photography industry has been active in the same way it is today. It's also difficult to predict how changes in the demands of customers will change in the next 10 years (e.g. if 3D photography was introduced, this may significantly reduce the demand for traditional stock photography).

[8] If we extend this model and assume that each image is capable of producing income for 10 years, before it no longer sells. If you never produced any photographs after the initial 10-year period, the portfolio would continue to generate earnings for the following 10 years, having made a total of $120,000.

10-Year Cumulative income

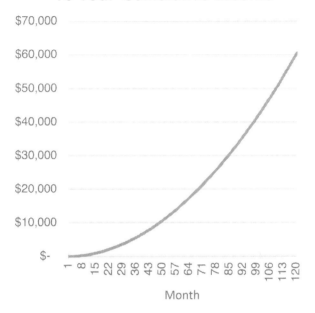

As you can see most of the generated earning s are incurred later on. In this model where the photographer is producing 100 images per month, just over $15,000 is produced in the first 5 years, but over $45,000 is produced in the last 5 years.

Stock photography can be lucrative over the long-term but will not make you a millionaire, and you cannot expect to receive your income immediately (this is a problem for new contributors, as it can take months to receive your first sale). It can take a long time for good images to become prominent in images searches, as popular images move higher in the search. It can also take a lot of time to find out what images sell well for you, and this will often take a lot of time and experimentation. Ultimately, it should be you ambition not to take great photos but to produce images that sell well over time.

Stock photography is a great way to produce passive income provided that you have a passion for passion for photography, which I know you have otherwise you wouldn't be reading this book. If you enjoy the creative process that comes with photography then the work involved will not feel like work, and you'll be making long term earnings through your hobby. Many people are interested in passive income because they don't enjoy the monotony of a 9-5 existence, and while this may or may not be you, secondary forms of income provide you with a greater sense of financial security in case you ever need to leave your job. If you are looking to take a step back from your current job, stock photography can provide you with the additional security and the skills you need to enter the photography industry and become your own boss.

How to get started in stock photography

Photography is an industry that is both artistic and technical. This requires both the necessary equipment and the appropriate skills and knowledge to make the most of your shots. In this section we will be going over what is necessary for a photographer to be able to not only enter the stock photography market, but to produce images that will compete well in the marketplace. While not all of the equipment mentioned in this section is necessary for all photographers, many pieces of equipment will be specialist and will help you to enter photography niches where there is less competition and greater earning potential.

As a beginner to stock photography it can seem like there is a lot of equipment that is required to enter the photography market, but this isn't really true. The bare minimum that's required is a relatively good camera, and some basic photo editing software[9]. A good way to manage the cost of buying new equipment is to only spend your earnings on new equipment. This can dent your earnings early on and may mean that you reach

---

[9] There are some viable applications that can be downloaded for free.

other market areas later, but it's a good way for you to learn to use your equipment one piece at a time, and to make sure that your business is making you, and not costing you, money.

Equipment

Camera

Your DSLR will become your new best friend.

Your camera is the only piece of equipment that you really need to start producing profitable stock photography. There is no requirement for the camera to be new, there are many used and refurbished cameras that are available for sensible prices that are appropriate for use in stock photography. As a general rule, most professional cameras made within the last 5 years will be sufficient for use in stock photography. While cheaper cameras are acceptable for stock photography, more expensive cameras will give the user better resolution, overall image quality and greater control over the image, however these advantages are bonuses and not requirements. For an entry-level camera, the only necessities are that your camera has interchangeable lenses and at least 12 megapixels.

When purchasing a camera, it may be worth considering the cost of purchasing just a 'body' (a camera without a lens), and purchasing the lens separate. This will give you greater control over your photography set-up and may avoid costs if you are planning to upgrade your lens in the future.

With modern advances in smartphone technology you may be tempted to use its camera to take your images in the beginning. This is not recommended, as the quality and control that you have over your image will not produce the standard that will sell well though stock agencies. The main issue being the sizes of the lenses and sensors, while acceptable for casual photography it will not be appropriate for stock images. Some agencies even use programs to detect images that have been taken on smartphones, and even if your photos are accepted, they will not compete well with the other images that have been taken with a good camera.

DSLR or mirrorless?

There are advantages to both kinds of camera, but broadly speaking mirrorless cameras will tend to be on the cheaper and lower-quality end of the spectrum. Mirrorless cameras do not contain many of the internal mechanisms contained in a DSLR which makes them cheaper and lighter than its DSLR equivalent. Mirrorless cameras do not allow you to see the through directly through the lens of the camera, and this can make it harder to judge the quality of your image, especially in low light. The best cameras that you can buy will be DSLRs, but you only need an entry-level camera to start producing stock photography and purchasing a modern mirrorless camera does come with significant cost advantages.

Lenses

The quality of an image will always be limited by the lens used. Lenses are useful for a variety of different reasons and allows the photographer to adapt to different situations and challenges. If you get to the point in which you wish to buy additional lenses, then it is recommended that you invest in good quality lenses. Lenses do not suffer from being outdated in the same way as cameras, as they technology they are based on is essentially constant, therefore a good lens, if treated correctly, is likely to outlast the camera it is bought for.

When buying lenses, it is advised that you do not purchase kit lenses, or that you upgrade from your kit lens as soon as possible. Kit lenses are the lenses that they typically come with a DSLR. While they are generally effective, their quality

21

can be limiting to a photographer. These will typically be the 18-55mm lenses that come with the DSLR and will be made of lower quality and cheaper materials.

Macro lens

Despite being very specialised, close-up shots like this are simply impossible with regular kit lenses and require a macro lens.

A typical kit lens will be able to focus on a subject that is at least 25cm away from the lens. In order to take images where the subject is closer, and more magnified, a macro lens is required. Macro lenses allows the photographers to focus on very small subjects or subjects that would ordinarily be too close to photograph as intended. Macro lenses can significantly increase your range as a photographer and should be considered once you've begun to experience sales in your stock portfolio.

Macro lenses are useful for:

- Flowers
- Jewellery
- Insects and nature
- Mechanical components

Telephoto lens

You don't always want to get close to your subject to photograph it.

Telephoto lenses do the opposite of macro lenses, that is they are useful for taking photographs of subjects that are far away. Telephoto lenses are the large lenses that you will have seen being used by professional photographers at sports matches and on wildlife documentaries, this is because a good quality telephoto lens has the ability to capture a subject from a long distance, when it wouldn't be appropriate to photograph it up close[10].

Telephoto lenses do not always need to be used to zoom in on a specific subject from a distance, but instead can be useful when capturing landscapes or cityscapes. The unique property of telephoto lenses means that the distances between objects that are closer or further from the camera appear to be reduced, giving an overall flatter appearance. Even at close distance this property can be used to produce more representative (and flattering) images of people.

Telephoto lenses are useful for:

- Sport
- Wildlife
- Portraiture
- Cityscapes

---

[10] E.g. a photographer cannot shoot on the pitch, or get close to an animal to photograph it.

Wide-angle lens

Wide-angle lenses give the photographer greater flexibility when framing the shot. The use of this lens allows the photographer to take a much wider image from the same location. This also emphasises the distance between objects in the foreground and the background.

Wide-angle lenses are just that, they capture the image at a wide angle. While it can be difficult to tell if an image has been taken with a wide-angle lens, it is a tool that gives the photographer more flexibility. Using a wide-angle lens, a photographer is able to capture more of the shot from one location (without having to step backwards). Wide-angle lenses also have the property of exaggerating the distance between elements that are closer or further from the camera.

Wide-angle lenses are useful for:

- Landscapes
- Architecture

Fish-eye lens

Fish-eye lenses create that unique look where the world seems to wrap around itself.

Fish eye lenses are a type of wide-angle lens, and are often referred to as ultra-wide-angle lenses. These lenses produce images that have such a wide angle of view that the image becomes heavily distorted and gives it the iconic fish-eye look. These images do not have any significant appeal in stock photography and are more appropriate for types of artistic photography but requires an honourable mention as you will most likely come across these when searching for new lenses.

Fish-eye lenses are useful for:

- Artistic photography

Speedlight

Speedlights are adjustable external flashes that fit into your camera's hotshoe. These provide additional light and are very useful when photographing people or in dark conditions. These can be bought relatively inexpensively and will offer greater flexibility than the flash that is built into your camera.

Tripod

A tripod will be one of the first additional pieces of equipment you will buy as you become more experienced in stock photography. This will be useful for photos where you want to maximise the quality of the image, by reducing the amount of movement when shooting, or to make sure the camera is exactly where you want it to be.

A tripod is important for:

▪ Reducing the amount of blur in an image.
▪ Ensuring that the camera is in the same position for multiple images.
▪ Ensuring the camera is at a specific height or angle.

Home studio set-up

Creating a studio in your own home is now cheaper and easier than it has ever been, and this will be attractive to those who want to produce images of isolated objects, one of the best-selling areas of stock photography. A home studio set-up will focus on creating an area with a white backdrop and bright white lighting.

Infinity curve

An infinity curve is a background (usually white) that reaches from the top to the base of the studio with no seams or edges, this give the effect of the subject existing in isolation. The cost of an infinity curve depends on the size of the set-up. For small objects a large white sheet of paper that is suspended at one end will be enough to create a seamless background. If you want to photograph people, this will require a more substantial set-up and enough room in your home to fit it.

Stationary lighting

Lighting is very important when photographing your subject in a studio. One of the issues is that the light you use has to be a pure white. Many home lamps have bulbs that produce a softer yellow light that is not appropriate for stock photography. The lighting you require will depend on the size of your subject and your studio. Small subjects, such as isolated objects, may only require one or two lamps with pure white bulbs installed. If you have a set-up that's arranged to photograph people, this may require much larger lights with diffusing screens and reflectors to soften the light on the subject.

Lightbox

A lightbox combines the infinity curve and lighting in one box that is small enough to fit on a desk. These are very inexpensive[11] and will be suitable for most beginners to stock photography. While they will not be large enough to photograph people, they are an excellent way to have a dedicated space for photographing small objects.

---

[11] Some lightbox set-ups are available online for less than $10.

The drawbacks are that these only allow for small objects to be photographed, and there is little control over the lighting. But due to their ease of use and low cost, this is a highly recommended purchase for beginners to stock photography.

Drone

Aerial images such as these are only possible with drone photography, but provides a unique perspective compared to a handheld camera.

Drone photography is one of the hottest trends in the stock photography industry. Only in the last few years have drones been a viable option for photography, and this has sparked an opportunity for stock contributors. The issue is that drone photography has one of the highest barriers to entry, that is the cost of the drone, not to mention also having the skill to operate it. Drone piloting is a skill in itself and is required to get value from drone photography. Similarly, the cost of a drone that's suitable for photography is at least $500. The other risk is that as drone technology gets better, the cost will go down resulting in their being many more drone photographers, if that happens then the above average sales in aerial photography would move towards average earnings. This should only really be considered by photographers that are already interested in drones, as it would take many sales to recover the expenditure of purchasing this expensive piece of equipment.

Accessories

As with any passion, photography comes with a wide range of accoutrements that at first seem unnecessary and later feel vital.

Memory card

Most photographers exclusively use external storage to save their images, typically on SD cards. Modern SD cards can hold many high-quality images and are reasonably affordable. More expensive SD cards will have more memory and a faster write speeds, however these are most useful for high-end photography and video recording. Nevertheless, it is always useful for a photographer to have a spare card on hand in one is lost, stops working or is needed in the heat of the moment.

Lens Hood

A lens hood is another tool that is used to prevent unwanted glare in the image. This works by only allowing light in the direction of the subject to enter the camera. This also acts as another form of protection for the lens.

White balance tools

White balance is essential to get the colouration right on your images and can be difficult to remedy in postproduction. A common tool for getting the white balance just right is a grey card, these are relatively inexpensive pieces of plastic set to 18% grey. When using a custom white balance setting, the camera will know that the card is the specific shade of grey and will calibrate accordingly.

Alternatively, some photographers recommend the use of an ExpoDisc, which works by adjusting the light balance using the camera's internal light meter to measure the colour temperature of light passing through the ExpoDisc to make an "in-camera" colour adjustment.

Filters

There are a wide variety of filters that photographer can experiment with. Coloured filters are not very useful to a stock photographer as any major adjustments to the colour can be done in post processing. Filters that are useful to stock photographer are neutral density (ND) filters, and polarising filters.

ND filters are useful because they reduce the overall amount of light that enters the camera, but do not change the colour of the image. This is useful because it allows photographers to increase the exposure time of the photograph, which produces a higher quality image.

Polarising filters are also popular with photographers because they remove glare from a photograph. This has the effect of making skies look darker and water clearer. These filters also help in managing harsh reflections in images.

Remote trigger

Remote triggers are used to take a photo without using the physical trigger on the camera. Using the trigger causes vibrations that my affect the quality of your image, a remote trigger will plug into your camera directly and can be used without touching the camera. Remote triggers can be either wired or wireless and are almost always used with tripods in order to reduce the amount of vibration.

Camera bag

Cameras are big investments, and it's always useful to have a case that can protect them from damage. Larger camera bags come with pockets and compartments to hold many different lenses, and different accessories. A camera bag is extremely useful when on a dedicated shoot.

Software

Photography is a skillset that has two parts. The first is the ability to take excellent photographs, this is both a technical and creative exercise. The second part is the post production, and this separates the good from the great photographs and is an essential skill for all photographers. Many photographers can be quite lazy in this area; either they do not want to edit the photographs at all, or they want to do minimal edits to a whole group of images in batch editing. Developing your skills in post processing is a way to make your images stand out and beat the competition. After all, if you're going to buy the appropriate equipment and learn how to take amazing photographs it only makes sense that you should spend those final moments perfecting the results of your craft. As mentioned before excellent editing is essential for making your photos stand out. Many of the best-selling images on Shutterstock will be very heavily processed, even to the point that many photographers would consider to be too-much. Nevertheless, being able to get your photo just right for your customer in the editing stage will be worth the additional time invested when compared with the extra earnings generated.

When discussing the software available to photographers, all conversations will eventually come back to two words: Photoshop and Lightroom. These are by far the industry leaders, to the point where professional photographers really do not consider using anything else. At the time of writing Adobe offers both Photoshop and Lightroom as a package for $10 per month. While this is a no-brainer for professional photographers, you will have to consider whether investing in these products is right for you as they will required that you produce an extra $120 per year in order to justify the cost.

Photoshop

Even though the difference is subtle, you can notice how the image to the right somehow feels more real. The right half of the image has been adjusted to make the image closer to what would be perceived by the human eye in real life.

Photoshop is the world's number 1 photo editing software; it's used by photographers all over the world because it is very versatile and is always being updated with new tools. Also, because it's the most popular there are many tutorials and forums available that help you to get the most out of this application.

The versatility of photoshop means that it is very useful for making your image look just how you want it to. As such it has a number of tools that are convenient for removing identifiable logos and faces from images, as well as a whole host of tools for creating composite images.

It is also possible to use pre-sets when editing your photos. These are specific settings that you can use to give your photos a particular look or feel that is consistent across many of your photos. It is common to see photographers selling their pre-sets online. Once you're comfortable with the stock photography model, selling pre-sets for photoshop is another way to make money passively through photography.

Lightroom

Lightroom is a very important tool and may be the reason why you choose to invest in the Adobe Photoshop and Lightroom package. Lightroom is used as a method of managing your database of images and is the application that many photographers use for batch processing. As you develop as a stock photographer and produce thousands of images, it can become difficult to keep track of your portfolio and to process you image efficiently. Lightroom is very useful in this respect as it is possible to edit many images at the same time, which can be very time efficient when applying the same processes to multiple images all taken on the same shoot under similar conditions. If working on a large scale, this massive time saving can be well worth the subscription.

Alternatives

While Photoshop and Lightroom are the best photo editing applications available, there are others, and this can create some cost savings when working with images in smaller quantities. Software companies such as Affinity produce photo editing and illustration software at a one-off price, at approximately $50. There may also be some free photo editing applications available, but these cannot really be recommended. If you are comfortable with the cheaper software, this may be suitable for you, but there is a reason why most professional photographers prefer Adobe.

Photography training

This guide has been written to help beginners to stock photography understand the industry and to help avoid many of the mistakes that come with the learning experience. It is beyond the scope of this book to give general photography advice, and if this is something that you feel you need there are many very good books on the subject. As such it is assumed that you have a reasonable understanding of photography before you begin. It is not required that you have a degree in photography but being familiar with the concepts such as composition and image processing will help you to produce professional quality images. As with any skill or craft it's essential that you master the rules before you go on to break them.

If you are not confident in your skills as a photographer, then there are plenty of resources that you can access on the internet free of charge that will be able to take you from an absolute beginner to a photography master. A very good source for tutorials on photography is YouTube: it is a free resource that is full of useful classes on photography skills and there are many blogs dedicated to the trends and developments within stock photography. There are also many stock photography forums which can be useful for learning from and keep engaged with the stock photography community.

As you develop as a stock photographer you may find that you wish to specialise in a particular niche. It is always useful to research your niche and see if there are other photographers that also specialise in your niche and have advice on how to improve.

How to create stock photography that sells

Stock photography can be very engaging because you can always tell when you really have a very good image because it will sell well. People vote with their wallets and will only purchase your photographs if they think they are good[12]. This is a good thing because it gives you perfectly honest feedback as to what works and what doesn't (and it can really surprise you as to what sells well). This also lets you know what areas you're strong in, and which you're not suited to. This is very useful when deciding what you want to spend your time photographing and how to increase your overall earnings per image.

When many photographers begin to sell stock photography, they enter the "ducks in the pond" phase. This involves shooting whatever is close to hand (such as household objects, pets, and ducks in the pond). Needless to say, many photographers go through this phase and for this reason Shutterstock is full of poor-quality images of ducks in ponds.

---

[12] Even if your mom says she likes your photos, if they don't sell then they probably aren't very good.

The one thing to always remember in stock photography is that images are needed for many varied purposes, so anything that you find interesting will probably be appealing to someone else. The great thing is that that stock images do not need to have mass appeal to be successful. Many mainstream markets are oversaturated, and many niche markets are undersupplied. Your images may also be serving a trend or market that doesn't exist yet[13], so even if your images do not sell well initially, they may have a boost in popularity later for an unexpected reason.

Ultimately, stock photography is a numbers game and even with a portfolio that has a high earnings per image, you will never out compete a large portfolio (on the condition that your images are of good quality). The good news is that digital photography is cheap, and that batch processors such as Lightroom allow you to maximise the number of images you can process in a given time. Because of this, always be on the lookout for overperforming images, and don't be afraid to experiment or diversify.

---

[13] For example, if your grandad left you his stamp collection, you may decide to create a stock image of the collection. This may not sell well initially, but images of stamps may be useful for an article about a resurgence in stamp collecting, or changes to the postal system.

General Rules

In this section we will cover some of the most successful categories for stock photography, but there are a few rules that are applicable to almost all images.

Just remember, while these rules are just general advice, don't be afraid to break them if you feel that you produce a better image because of it. Eventually you will come up with your own rules which may look different to these.

1. Take photographs at the same level as the subject.

   While this can be difficult for very large or very small subjects, it is always best to try to take your image so that you are aligned horizontally to your subject. This has the effect of psychologically removing the distance between the subject and the viewer. This also creates the 'look' that people expect from stock photography.

2. Shoot the same subject at different times of the day and under different light conditions.

   If shooting outdoors, it can be very useful to try shooting a subject at different times of the day. The best times to shoot outdoors are in the early mornings and late evenings[14]. Capturing the same shot at dawn, midday, dusk and night will give you several differentiated shots of the same subject.

3. Make sure your background is sellable.

   Having the right subject is always very important but the factor that may see a customer buying from your competitor rather than you may be your image's background. Customers will need your images for a variety of purposes, and if the background doesn't match their needs, they may choose another image over yours, even if your competitor has a poorer overall image.

4. Try to produce differentiated images.

   While most stock photographers want to maximise the size of their portfolios, you can achieve a more lucrative portfolio of the same size by producing images that other photographers do not. This can be done by taking advantage of any interests or expertise that you have[15], or by making

---

[14] Also known as the "golden hours", the first hour of daylight after sunrise and the last hour of sunlight before sunset provide golden light with long shadows which is amazing for any outdoor photography.
[15] If you have an interest or hobby this can be a great source of images. If you enjoy rock-climbing or SCUBA diving, take

the most of what's in your local area. Try to use what's available and do not incur extra costs by buying things to shoot.

5. Perfect your images in postprocessing

Almost no image comes out of the camera without the opportunity for improvement. It is often the photographers that can master both photography and postprocessing that become the most successful. That being said, even if it's only a batch process in Lightroom, almost all of your images will have more commercial viability after being processed.

---

images of people doing that. If it's interesting to you, it will be interesting to other people but not everyone will have access to these types of shots.

Popular categories

Food and drink

Here is an excellent photograph of a cup of coffee with a croissant. The background is clear and the creates focus on the subject.

The 'food and drink' category is very popular for stock photography and is an area in which you can generate decent earnings. One of the great opportunities that comes with this style of photography is that you can make the most of current food trends (e.g. vegan, organic, healthy etc.).

The main issue with this type of stock photography is that it is a crowded market, that doesn't mean it isn't profitable (as there is also a high demand), but it does mean that only high-quality images sell well. When you're photographing food a drink you have the opportunity to control every aspect of the photograph (lighting, composition, subject, postprocessing, etc.), because of this it is essential that the images are perfect as other photographers will be producing images that are. If you are able to create strong photographs in this area, then you will be able to compete effectively and generate sales consistently.

Tips and tricks
- You don't need to buy or prepare food especially for stock photography. Use what you already have in your kitchen.
- Find a location where you can control the lighting.
- Make sure that you make the food look delicious in post-production.
- Creating a 'food and drink' photo with a lot of blank (or negative) space is useful for designers that want to use the image as a background.
- DO NOT take photos on your smartphone of food that you eat in restaurants. The overall quality (lighting and composition) of the image will not be good enough and will only result in rejections or stock that does not sell.

Cityscapes

No other shot represents the French capital quite like the iconic Eiffel tower. It's also a great example of the importance of copyright when photographing cities: While the tower itself is not protected by copyright, the lights on its surface are, therefore photographs of the Eiffel tower at night cannot be sold.

Cityscapes are another popular yet competitive area for stock photography. The difficulty with cityscapes is that large and important cities have some of the best-selling images and come with the challenges of competing with many very good photographs. As a general rule, the most successful stock photographs in this category will be of major cities, and in particular, iconic buildings. Iconic buildings can be very useful for a stock photographer, especially those that would be relevant to common news articles[16].

---

[16] Images of the New York stock exchange are useful for American financial news, whereas photographs of the Bank

Shooting the same buildings from different angles at different times of the day or under different types of light can be very useful and will create a good portfolio of images that will create long lasting income.

Every city will have some value and it can be useful to capture images that are unique to your local city (e.g. the city flag, town hall, an iconic town square or building). Try to avoid generic cityscapes that are unrecognisable and could be of any city; this market is already saturated and even good quality images cannot compete.

Holiday destinations are also a viable market within cityscapes. Many advertising agencies will use images of regular holiday destinations, and so these images are always in demand. While it is not recommended that you go on holiday in order to take these photographs, it can be useful to spend an hour or two in a day taking photographs which you can process when back home and can reduce the overall cost of your holiday.

As mentioned before there is potential to produce sellable images of cities but this is on the condition that the images are perfect. This is a competitive field and while there is the potential

---

of England or British Houses of Parliament are useful for British political news.

for good long-term earnings, the composition, lighting and postproduction need to be high-quality to penetrate this market.

IMPORTANT: Stock photography agencies will not accept images that contain identifiable:

- Logos
- Faces
- License plates

These will only be accepted in editorial submissions, otherwise all of these will need to be removed from your images in postproduction. It is also important to note that some buildings come under copyright and images of them cannot be sold. A famous example of this is the Eiffel tower; while the tower itself is not copyrighted, the lights that cover it are protected by copyright, therefore you will be unable to sell images of the Eiffel tower at night.

Tips and tricks

- Images that sell well are those that define a location.
- Ensure that there are no identifiable logos, faces or license plates in your images.
- While it can be a great way to mitigate some of the costs involved with travel, it is unlikely that you can recover the costs of a holiday through stock photography.

Landscape

This is an excellent landscape image: Firstly, the identifiable mount Fuji instantly makes you think of Japan or nearby Tokyo. Secondly the soft colour palate and golden light gives the photograph a sense of calm. It is this mix of composition and subject matter that gives the shot its effectiveness.

Landscapes are another crowded area, but a great photo can sell very well and produce good returns for years to come. The great thing about landscape photography is that you won't run into any of the copyright issues that affect some of the other popular categories. The quality of the image will mostly come down to the emotional quality that the image has; if a particular landscape image speaks to you or provides you with a strong emotion (such as awe, beauty or calm), then it's likely to appeal to other people as well.

Just be careful of the "photos on a hike" issue, while going on a hike may be the perfect time to take great landscape photos, this is the same for everyone else and while most of these will not be good shots, if you can produce images that are well composed and postprocessed, and it contains and emotional quality to it, then these photographs can create consistent returns to the stock photographer.

Concept

What does this image say to you? The map and camera may remind you of travel, the photographs and journal may make you think of a writer that has a story to tell after an adventure.

Concept photography centres on the idea of using images to demonstrate a certain intangible idea or concept. This can be an area of stock photography that creates good earnings for the contributor if they can create an image that effectively conveys the idea they're trying to create. For this type of photography, it can be useful to find several objects and to arrange them in such a way that it creates a certain mood or presents a certain concept that a designer may want to represent.

Images under this category do not necessarily have to be a collection of objects, but only need to be representative of an idea. These do not have to be broad concepts, and in many ways niche images can avoid a lot of competition. Good examples of concept photography may include:

- Passports and tickets on a map, to represent travel.
- A car covered in snow, to represent travel disruption.
- A picture of weights, water, and a skipping rope on a gym floor, to represent sport and fitness.

The image should create a certain "feel' or provide definite symbolism. The closer to the theme your image is, the more attractive it will be to potential customers.

Composite photography

This incredible image of the different phases of the moon could never exist in real life but is possible through the use photo-editing.

Composite photography relies on the photographer's photo-editing a postprocessing skills. This is an area in which a stock photographer can enter those less-crowded niches. Many designers are looking for the convenience to create the product that they want without expending additional time and effort, others still don't have the necessary technical knowledge to create these impressive composite images. As a photographer with strong postprocessing or illustrating skills there is a potential to create the images and illustrations that customers want but can't, or don't want, to create themselves.

Composite photography could be considered to be in the same category as concept photography as the purpose of both styles is to convey an idea or concept visually. Composite photography differs as the photographer is creating an image that could never exist in real life, but nonetheless demonstrates an idea that the designer is trying to convey. This can even include very ordinary images that are supplemented with additional objects in the composition[17].

Don't be afraid to be creative with composite photography, all images will be a work of fantasy and cannot exist in real life, but this does not mean that the image needs to be complicated in order to be appealing to customers. Good examples of composite photography may include:

- Images of people thinking or interacting with objects, with illustrations that help explain their moods or thoughts.
- Images of impossible scenes (e.g. a sunset with 2 or 3 moons, or a horn on a horse to make a unicorn).
- Writing text, or inserting another image, on a blank page, book, poster, laptop.

Be creative but try to see the value the image would have for the customer.

---

[17] For example, an image of someone thinking, a question mark above their head may symbolise confusion, a lightbulb above their head may symbolise an idea.

Aerial

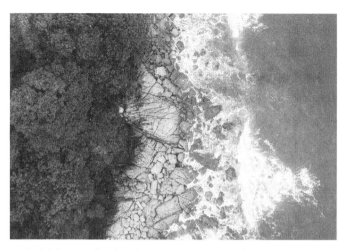

Aerial photography gives the opportunity to look at the familiar from a completely new angle.

Aerial photography has become very popular in recent years as drones have become much more accessible. This area of photography can be very lucrative for stock photographers as the level of competition in this field is not as intense as in many of the more accessible areas of photography. The benefits of being in this market are caused by the high barrier to entry, which is owning a drone with a camera that is good enough for stock photography. This can be very expensive and is the reason why many photographers do not invest in these pieces of equipment. This creates a great opportunity for photographers that are willing to invest in the necessary equipment to take these photographs.

As an aerial photographer there is almost no limit to the number of amazing photographs that you can take. Almost any location has areas that will look amazing as an aerial image. If you own a drone, or would consider purchasing one, this can be a very profitable area of photography to enter.

IMPORTANT: The laws that govern the use of drones varies from country to country, and it is important to be clear about the local regulations where you live. In the USA, drone laws are fairly relaxed and are covered by federal law (so that same rules apply in each state). In Europe (and the rest of the world) regulations on drones will vary from country to country and may be difficult research.

Backgrounds

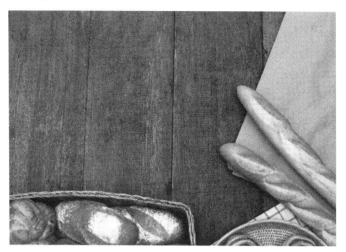

This image provides the ideal background for a designer: The wooden background provides good contrast for white text; the bread and baskets tell us that rustic food or baking is at the heart of this message; and the large amount of free space gives the designer plenty of room to showcase their message.

Background images are a stock photographer's best friend. These images sell very well on the condition that they provide a good background for the designer to showcase their own information. These are needed all time by different types of designers for all sorts of purposes, including:

- Website backgrounds
- Flyers
- Adverts
- Presentations

Backgrounds for all subjects and styles are needed and these will be useful for those designers that are trying to complement their message with photography. What customers are looking for in this area is for the image to have a lot of free (or negative) space in which they can display their message, logo, or information. While it is not necessary to include additional objects into the image, these can help provide the context that the background needs to be effective. This is an excellent reminder that the purpose of stock photography is not to produce beautiful photographs, but to provide images that are useful to the client.

Good examples of background photography include:

- Textured backgrounds that are useful to website backgrounds (e.g. stone, wood or wallpaper).
- Images that are mostly empty except for a few complimentary objects around the outside (e.g. a gym floor with a few weights and bottles around the outside or on one side of the image).
- An image with black space in a familiar setting (e.g. a blank piece of paper pinned onto a corkboard).

Seasons, holidays and events

One look at this picture will remind anyone of Christmas.

All throughout the year there are different events and holidays for which your customers will need photographs for. These photos sell very well, especially the more commercial holidays such as Christmas. This category could almost be called Christmas on its own but there are a whole host of seasons, holidays and events that you can take advantage of. While the aim of passive income is to create content that provides a regular income, exposure to seasonal stock photography will see your earnings peak around these events. While Christmas is definitely the biggest of these, diversifying into a lot of different holidays will help to secure a more regular income.

When looking to create stock photography that represents the holidays, the most sellable images are those which exclusively symbolise that holiday, in the way that a Christmas tree is only associated with Christmas, this creates a strong message for you image and it will make it more saleable. This technique can be used for almost all seasons, events or holidays. Good examples involve:

- Trees, gifts, baubles, candy canes etc. for Christmas.
- Pumpkins for both Halloween and Autumn.
- Red roses for Valentine's day.
- Shamrocks for St. Patrick's Day.

Try to remember that traditions and holidays vary from country to country, but the stock photography market is international. Try to make the most of the traditions you understand the best[18]. Taking photos of what is a part of your culture will give you access to those niches that will help your images stand out and sell well.

Don't forget that the same rules also apply to the seasons. Many companies will be using images that are associated with the current time of year, so try to take photos of what's relevant to you in your season. This can be a simple as taking

---

[18] For example, the British cannot imagine Christmas without crackers (popping cardboard tube with a toy and paper hat inside) and Christmas pudding, or Easter without chocolate eggs. Germans may not be able to imagine Christmas without gingerbread houses.

photographs of snowmen in the winter, cherry blossom in the spring, sunsets in the summer or trees full of brown leaves in the autumn.

Tips and tricks

- Try to take photographs of what you are exposed to during these seasons and holidays, the things you see the most will probably be what other people see a lot and will associate with that time of year.

- Use your seasonal items for your photography. This can mean that you are too late to take advantage of the benefits of this year, but it can be useful for next year. For example, if you have roses in your home after Valentine's day, photograph those roses and the images will be ready for sale for Valentine's day next year.

Isolated objects

What does this image symbolise? It could represent an idea, power,
electricity, light or it could just simply be a lightbulb.

Isolated objects are what most people think of
when they think of stock photography, and it's not
surprising as this is one of the best-selling areas
of stock photography; it is highly accessible and
very much in demand. If you are just starting in
stock photography this should be one of the areas
that you try to enter into first. This area of stock
photography is always very efficient for the
photographer because each image can be used
in many different ways, giving each photo the
opportunity to be used by many different
customers in a variety of ways.

With a little investment in a few pieces of home-
studio equipment you can create a set up that will
allow you to take images of objects with controlled
lighting and a seamless white background. These

images will form the core of your stock portfolio. As with other areas of stock photography, understanding your equipment and ensuring that the composition and postprocessing of your images is key.

Objects on a seamless white background sell the best. Black backgrounds are also appropriate where the object is white or doesn't photograph well on a white background (e.g. a transparent water bottle) but always try to use a white background where possible. Shadows and reflections are acceptable but try not to include any lighting that's too harsh.

This form of stock photography is very efficient to photograph and process, t therefore should make up most of your portfolio. Get creative, you never know what image will be useful for a customer, so when you're ready to photograph try to take photos of a wide variety of objects.

IMPORTANT: As with all other areas of stock photography, make sure that the object that you're photographing does not show any recognisable brand names or logos. Otherwise the image will only be usable as editorial.

Non-isolated objects

Game, set and match. This image can only mean one thing: Tennis.

Similar to isolated objects, non-isolated objects will try to demonstrate a specific concept of idea but with a background that also complements the object. While not as popular as isolated objects, this area of photography allows for more differentiation. The purpose of this is to create a stronger concept than would be possible with an object on a white background. Many people like isolated objects but these can appear very sterile, non-isolated objects provide a greater degree of context and look less like generic stock images.

This is an area of photography that sells moderately well and should be considered a complement to your stock portfolio.

Lifestyle and people

This image summaries the work of an architect in one image.

Stock photography that features people, also known as lifestyle photography, is one of the most lucrative areas of stock photography and will, on average, sell better than even images of isolated objects. The reason why this area of stock photography is so lucrative is because there are relatively fewer images that feature real people. Lifestyle photography is less competitive because it tends to involve other people that often need to be paid for their modelling services, or at least convinced to model for you. Because it's so much harder to take a get a person to pose for you than an inanimate object there are fewer images in this category, but this in turn creates an opportunity for the entrepreneur.

As with all stock photography, an image still needs to convey a concept even if there are people in it. If you use a model, or even a pet, make sure they are doing something interesting or they are expressing an emotion. Portraits on the whole are not very sellable, so ensure that there is a theme to your image, even if it's an image of someone thinking, smiling, or frowning. Reasonable acting skills are preferred.

One of the bestselling areas of lifestyle images is that which involves people working in specific professions, an image of a doctor in their scrubs or a judge in their robes will be much more marketable as these subjects have a wide appeal and a relatively small supply. If you know anyone that has a recognisable profession, it could be lucrative to ask to photograph them while they are in their uniform.

IMPORTANT: Whenever you photograph a person you will need a model release in order to be able to sell images that feature that person. Model releases require the signature of both the model and a witness. Model releases are available on the stock agencies website. Failure to include completed model release forms will result in the image being rejected.

Corporate

Graphs, laptops, clipboards and firm and a strong handshake. We know that these people mean serious business.

Corporate photography is big business. Every annual report, brochure or company presentation needs an image of some very happy people in suits doing some important business. While this area of stock photography could come under the heading of 'lifestyle', it really deserves its own mention as this is a very large section of the of the stock photography market. Most offices and businesses are actually very ordinary, which is why when businesses market themselves they like to use very clean, friendly and professional looking images to represent them. This creates a huge audience if you can create these images yourself and can be done very easily with either yourself or a volunteer model in a suit either looking friendly, pointing to a graph, writing on a board, or shaking hands.

This can be a difficult one to get right, but if you have access to this sort of environment you have the potential to create a very profitable stock portfolio. Profitable corporate photos include:

- People in suits smiling or shaking hands.
- People explaining graphs or giving presentations.
- Multi-ethnic groups in a corporate environment.
- People in suits looking friendly and shaking hands with clients.

Many of these scenarios sound very generic, but the professional world isn't very creative and so they like to use very bland and inoffensive images.

Postprocessing

The first part of producing images that sell well though stock agencies will be selecting the right subject matter and using your photography skills capture your image in a way that is commercially viable. After this you will need to focus on how you process your images to make them stand out from the competition. It goes without saying that there is strong competition in almost all areas of stock photography, so strong postprocessing skills are a must.

Batch editing

Batch editing will be the first step in refining your images. After a shoot, you will no doubt have many photos to process, and many duplicates of your images. Batch editing is useful for selecting which images you choose to delete, and which you wish to edit.

After you've chosen which images you wish to keep, you will want to edit the images you have taken on your shoot. It's usual to edit all images taken under the same light conditions in the same way. This can be done easily with software such as Lightroom.

Batch editing is a very general tool, and for many images you may choose to make edits to individual photos.

Photo editing

The photo editing stage is the final phase of the image creation process and involves making edits to individual images. This part of the procedure will typically include:

- Cropping
- Levels adjustment
- Applying metadata
- Applying effects
- Adjusting the background
- Removing identifiable logos, brands or faces

While this can be more time consuming, it is easiest to make the major adjustments to images in the batch processing phase and leaving only the final details for the photo editing phase.

Postprocessing is a skill in itself and it is important that you are confident in using these tools. It can often feel as if you can never stop making improvements to an image, but with stock photography there is a strong emphasis on producing volume and so you will need to develop the confidence to edit an image very quickly[19], without perfecting it.

---

[19] Some experienced stock photographers dedicate as little as an average of 30 seconds per image. This is what is required to work on the scale of a professional stock photographer. While this may not be recommended for beginners, you should seek to be able to spend as little time as possible editing your images.

How to optimise your stock photography process

At this point you should be confident about what stock photography is, be familiar with the equipment and software that many stock photographers use and understand what sort of images sell well though the stock agencies. This section of the audiobook aims to go over how you can manage your stock portfolio efficiently to produce more sales, and reduce the time spent on the administrative side of stock photography.

Stock photography is an industry that experiences fluctuations in sales and so when we've talked about average earnings on images, these should really be taken as averages over the long-term. Before you get involved in stock photography be aware that periods of poor sales do happen, in these periods it really helps if you have a passion for photography as this can get you through the difficult months. A well-diversified portfolio will help to reduce the impact of slow sales and listing your images with multiple stock agencies can increase sales and reduce some of the variation in monthly returns.

Stock Photography Agencies

Stock photography agencies are the intermediaries through which you will sell your images. As a new stock photographer, you may consider listing your work on as many stock photography websites as possible. While this makes perfect sense, it is not recommended as the time involved with listing on multiple sites will counteract the value of the extra sales that you will receive.

Some stock agencies may offer preferential rates of commission in exchange for being an exclusive contributor for their agency, but It is also not recommended that you accept an offer such as this. This type of arrangement is far too limiting, especially for beginners to stock photography, and you will want to increase, not limit, your maximum potential earnings. That being said, you will probably only want to list your images with 2 or 3 different agencies.

Shutterstock

www.shutterstock.com

Shutterstock is the largest stock agency in the world. It has over 250 million images in its database, with approximately 1.3 million being added weekly. This will most likely be your best-selling agency as a contributor.

Shutterstock is quite opaque in how it calculates the amount of revenue that you will receive for each sale. Shutterstock offers different subscription packages for its customers, and these will generate less royalties than single purchases, but will make up the majority of your sales. In addition to this the value of the commission that you receive for each subscription sale is dependent on the value of your total earnings with Shutterstock[20], meaning that you will generate higher rates of commission, as your earnings increase.

One of the major benefits of using Shutterstock is that the process for uploading and keywording your images is one of the easiest there is, and this makes the whole process relatively quick and easy. While the commission system may be opaque and complicated, most users report earnings of $0.50-0.80 per image download.

Fotolia

www.fotolia.com

Fotolia is the stock agency owned by Adobe, the producers of Photoshop and Lightroom. This agency has become much more popular in recent

---

[20] If you think this is complicated, it's because it is. This is no doubt an attempt by Shutterstock to disguise their payment structure. But as it's the biggest in the industry this will be difficult to avoid, so you will just have to accept what they give you.

years, and this is most likely because the microstock service has been integrated directly into their photo editing software.

Photography is not the core business of Adobe and so the system is not focused on contributors. As such the user interface is not as easy to use as that of Shutterstock, and this can be very noticeable when dealing with a large portfolio. A photographer can expect to receive $1-1.10 per image download.

iStock

www.istockphoto.com

iStock is owned by Getty images, one of the largest visual media companies in the world and is a favourite with many of the media outlets in the world. iStock also has a more complex upload system when compared to Shutterstock and Fotolia.

The earning rate for iStock is considered to be one of the lowest in the industry, average revenue will tend to be around $0.20-0.50 per image download. This seems low by comparison, but as mentioned before, iStock is very popular with media outlets and so the increase in sales will offset the reduction in earnings per download.

Other agencies

There are other agencies available to join, many of which will offer a greater amount of commission on each sale, but these tend to be much smaller and so you can expect fewer sales overall. The only major advantage of selling through a smaller agency is that there is less overall competition and so it is easier to rise higher in the searches.

Uploading to stock agencies can take a lot of time, so you do want to be selective in which agencies you invest your time into. A good idea is to experiment with which smaller agencies work for you[21]. Set a target for the total sales value of your submissions, and if the agency reaches these targets you might consider uploading with them regularly[22]. Also, if you do choose to list with a smaller agency, check in from time to time, small agencies go out of business regularly and you may find that your images are no longer for sale.

If you are considering listing with smaller agencies here are a few that may be useful:

---

[21] This is best done once you have more experience in selling stock photography as you will understand what 'normal' sales through the major agencies looks like.

[22] Be careful when listing with smaller stock agencies, some will promote your photos in the first few weeks to encourage more uploads, but this may not be representative of your long-term performance.

Pond5

www.pond5.com

An agency that is mostly focused towards stock footage submissions but does have a photography marketplace. This agency allows the contributor to set the price, and to keep 50% of that sale price. Do not expect a large amount of sales from this agency, so set your prices high as a result.

Stocksy

www.stocksy.com

Specialist in artistic stock photography. A very small agency that requires exclusivity on all submissions. It can be difficult to join, as the agency has a "call to artists" about once a year, when they allow new contributors but do not accept many.

Robert Harding

www.robertharding.com

Specialists in travel photography. Requires exclusivity but provides their contributors with briefs and gives feedback on content.

Metadata

Metadata relates to all the additional information attached to your image files that will be used by the search algorithms to direct customers to your images. Getting your metadata right is very important and is a skill in itself, but once you understand it, it will become an easy process.

Bear in mind that the search algorithms promote entries that are useful to the customer, therefore the more relevant you can make your keywords, the better your images will perform in searches, which is why you should think carefully before including keywords[23]. It is also recommended that you keep a spreadsheet that contains the metadata for all your images, especially when they are under review, as any rejections will mean that you will have to go through the keywording process all over again. When submitting your image, you will be required to input 3 key types of metadata; title, description and keywords.

Title

The title should contain the main keywords that you wish to promote and will give the customer a general indication about the subject of the image.

---

[23] Many of the most successful images in searches will use almost all of the available space in the title, description and keywords.

Description

The description should contain all of the information contained within the title, as well as any other important keywords that can be contained within the space for the description.

Keywords

Your keywords are the most important aspect of your metadata and should be treated as such. The keywords that you select will be very important as this is the information that the customers will use to find your work. There is not much transparency on how Shutterstock's search algorithm works, but we can assume that they work in a similar way to Google, who has the best search algorithms in the world, so techniques that work for Google should be suitable for Shutterstock.

When producing keywords for your images, try not to limit it to the name or description of your subject, include synonyms and related words to your metadata[24]. Customers are not always aware of what they want and may be more likely to search for the concept or emotion that they're looking for. It can always be useful to include not

---

[24] For example, if you have a picture of some fitness weights, include keywords such as "Dumbbell", "Barbell" as well as concepts such as "Fitness", "Bodybuilding" and "Muscle".

only what the image contains, but also how your image feels[25].

The opposite can also be true, a large part of Shutterstock customers will be made of professional designers and will be looking for specific and technical descriptors[26]. This is the opposite type of customer who knows exactly what they want including the details of the shooting conditions and the camera that took the image. Useful keywords may relate to:

- Type of light

  Day, night, indoor, studio.

- Angle

  Close-up, macro, high angle.

- People

  Caucasian, Asian, Multi-ethnic, no people.

- Isolated

  Isolated object, background, non-isolated.

---

[25] A customer that is involved in advertising or design may not search for "Mountain" but may search for "Adventure" or "Travel".
[26] Remember that different cultures have different spellings or terms that they use for the same thing. For example, what Americans would call a 'vacation', the British would call a 'holiday'. Similarly, the colour 'grey' is written as 'gray' in American English.

- Location[27]

  Place names, country, district, city.

Tools

While deciding the appropriate keywords for an image may be difficult, there are a few tools that may help you to select profitable keywords:

- Microstock group keyword tool

  microstockgroup.com/tools/keyword.php

  A tool that will show you images that are similar to the keywords that you describe, and recommends popular keywords based on the images you select. Highly recommended.

- Shutterstock suggestions

  Shutterstock has very good algorithms and will be able to suggest some fairly accurate keywords based on similar images.

Rejections

While it's annoying and inefficient to experience rejections, all are avoidable. Try to remember that all stock agencies want to list your images and

---

[27] Alternative and local location names can be useful in keywording. A non-German speaker may search for "German parliament building" whereas a German speaker would search for "Reichstag". Similarly, a non-Dutch speaker may search for "Netherlands" whereas a Dutch speaker would search for "Nederland".

won't reject your images unless there is no real prospect of them selling. If you follow the guidelines laid out in this book, rejections should not be a common problem. Nevertheless, rejections will be based on one or more of the following issues:

- Quality
- Subject matter
- Metadata

Quality

The quality of the image was not good enough for sale. This is very common when the image has been taken with a smartphone. This can also happen when the appropriate steps in taking the photo or in production have not been taken to ensure a high-quality image. Hopefully this will not be an issue, but if you do get a rejection based on quality, try to identify at which part of process the problems occurred and try to avoid these in the future. Issues can fall under the following categories:

- Focus
- Noise
- Exposure

Subject matter

The subject matter itself is subject to copyright or there is some legal issue as to why the image cannot be sold. This will be relevant if an image is submitted that contains a brand or logo, or an identifiable face is included without including a complete model release. As mentioned before these images are inappropriate for stock photography. For this you will either have to obtain the appropriate model release or remove all identifiable brands, logos, or faces, depending on what's required. If this is an issue that cannot be remedied you may consider selling these images under editorial, rather than not at all. Issues can fall under the following categories:

- Missing or invalid model release
- Intellectual property
- Non-licensable content
- Trademark

Metadata

This is a rejection based on poor keywording or significant English language or grammar error in the keywords and description. While this can be an issue for non-native English speakers, the keywording tools mentioned above can help to avoid this. Issues can fall under the following categories:

- Keywords
- Image titles
- Spelling & grammar

Final notes

This book was produced to teach you about the fundamentals of the passive income model, and how this can be applied to stock photography. We have also covered the necessary equipment that you will need in order to produce stock photography effectively, as well as the areas of stock photography that are most profitable for contributors. Finally, we discussed how to optimise the stock photography process to create a more efficient and profitable stock portfolio. You now have all the information that you require to start producing profitable stock photography and an effective passive income stream.

We hope that you have enjoyed this book.

For more editions just like this please search 'Abstract Press'.

Original text by Jett Parker-Holland, 2019.

ABSTRACT PRESS

Made in the USA
Middletown, DE
13 October 2024

62535450R00061